LET ME FALL APART

A LIFE IN POETRY

JASON P INGLESTON

LET ME FALL APART

Copyright ©JASON INGLESTON 7709 PUBLISHING 2022

All rights reserved

The characters and events portrayed in this book are fictitious. Any similarity to real persons, living or dead is coincidental and not intended by the author.

No part of this book may be reproduced, or stored in a retrieval system, or transmitted in any form or by any means, electronic, mechanical, photocopying, recording, or otherwise, without express written permission of the publisher.

ISBN- 9798847403993

LET ME FALL APART

FOREWORD

I WRITE BECAUSE IT'S A RELEASE OF MY STRUGGLES AND NO MATTER WHERE WE ARE IN LIFE OR HOW WE GOT THERE WE HAVE THINGS TO OVERCOME. SO CELEBRATE YOUR ACHIEVEMENTS AND LEARN FROM YOUR FAILURES, BECAUSE AS LONG AS THERE'S A BREATH IN YOUR LUNGS AND A BEAT IN YOUR HEART THEN THERE IS STRENGTH TO BELIEVE IN YOURSELF.

LET ME FALL APART

LET ME FALL APART

I'D LIKE TO THANK SOME IMPORTANT PEOPLE IN MY LIFE. FIRST OF ALL MY DAUGHTER SAGE WHO IS MY ROCK, I LOVE YOU SO MUCH AND I'M PROUD OF THE PERSON YOU'VE BECOME. A THANK YOU TO MY CLOSE FRIEND ERICA SALA WHO HAS HELPED WITH A LOT IN THE WRITING & EDITING PROCESS AS WELL IN LIFE. TO MY PARENTS, FAMILY AND FRIENDS I CAN'T THANK YOU ALL ENOUGH FOR YOUR UNDYING SUPPORT AND LOVE.

LET ME FALL APART

THERE ARE PEOPLE OUT THERE THAT CAN SIT FOR HOURS

NO CONVERSATIONS AT ALL

JUST THEIR BREATH AND IMAGINATION

NO OUTSIDE NOISE OR DISTRACTIONS

A BEAUTIFUL LIGHT SHINING IN THEIR ENDLESS LOVE

OF WONDER AND CONTENT

PIECE OF MIND IS FREE

BUT PIECE OF SOUL IS RARE

LET ME FALL APART

OUR DAYS ARE NUMBERED

SO NEVER LET ANYONE CONTROL THE COUNT

LET ME FALL APART

IF YOU DON'T KEEP MOVING FORWARD

YOU'LL ALWAYS BE CLOSER TO YOUR PAST

LET ME FALL APART

THAT CONTROL ONLY EXISTS BECAUSE YOU LET FEAR

CONTROL YOU!

READ THAT AGAIN!

LET ME FALL APART

EVERYTIME YOU LIED TO ME

I WISH YOU COULD HAVE TOLD THE TRUTH

SO MAYBE I COULD TOO

LET ME FALL APART

SOME PEOPLE WANT TO LIVE THEIR LIFE

JUST NOT ALONE

LET ME FALL APART

AND THAT DAY WILL COME WHEN MY MEMORY

OF YOU WILL BE LONGER THAN I KNEW YOU AND

MY BREATHS WITH YOU WILL BE FAR LESS THAN THE ONES WITHOUT YOU

LET ME FALL APART

I ALWAYS WANTED US TO GROW

I JUST DIDN'T REALIZE IT WOULD BE APART

LET ME FALL APART

THE TRUTH ONLY HURTS

IF YOU DON'T WANT TO BELIEVE IT

LET ME FALL APART

MAY YOU GET PAST YOUR PAST

LET ME FALL APART

YOU LIE TO YOURSELF OUT OF FEAR

I LIE TO MYSELF OUT OF LOVE

WE ARE NOT THE SAME!

LET ME FALL APART

BE MORE RESPONSIBLE WITH OTHER PEOPLES HEARTS

LET ME FALL APART

MAY YOU FALL IN LOVE WITH THE WORDS

AND STAY FOR THE MOMENTS

LET ME FALL APART

SOMETIMES FEAR WILL KEEP YOU AWAY

FROM EVERYTHING YOU LOVE

BUT IT'S LOVE THAT CAN KEEP YOU SAFE FROM

EVERYTHING YOU FEAR

LET ME FALL APART

DON'T BE ATTACHED TO THE OUTCOME

FALL IN LOVE WITH THE STORY

LET ME FALL APART

IN A 3 A.M. SLOW DANCE HE WHISPERED

"I HOPE YOU UNDERSTAND THAT WHAT LIFE HAS TO OFFER YOU,

IS FAR GREATER THAN WHAT IT HAS TAKEN AWAY"

LET ME FALL APART

THERE ARE PEOPLE WHO READ HALF THE BOOK

AND THINK THEY KNOW THE WHOLE STORY

LET ME FALL APART

THOSE WHO RUN TO REDEMPTION

KNOW THAT TEMPTATION ISN'T FAR BEHIND

LET ME FALL APART

IVE SEEN YOU WRITE A BEAUTIFUL STORY THEN BURN THE PAGE

HOLD EVERYTHING AROUND YOU WITH LOVE & WATCH IT TURN INTO RAGE

UNBREAKABLE SPIRIT BUT DRIVEN BY DEMONS DEDICATED TO SELF SABOTAGE

THE PARALLELS OF DEPRESSION SEE HAPPINESS AS A MIRAGE

THE LIGHT IN LIFE SCATTERED WITHIN GLIMPSES OF HOPE

GETTING THROUGH IT IS A MAZE & FIGURING OUT HOW TO COPE

ALL THE THINGS I KNOW YOU CAN NOT BARE

BUT ALWAYS KNOW WE TRIED TO TAKE YOU FAR AWAY FROM THERE

LET ME FALL APART

A LITTLE BIT OF LETTING GO

CAN LEAD TO A LOT OF UNDERSTANDING

LET ME FALL APART

LIFE IS NOT ALWAYS A FAIRY TALE

SOMETIMES YOU GET EATEN BY THE DRAGON

LET ME FALL APART

SOMETIMES THE REGRET LASTS LONGER THAN THE LESSON

LET ME FALL APART

THE HARDEST PART WAS FIGURING OUT

HOW MY LIFE WORKED AGAIN WITHOUT YOU

LET ME FALL APART

FIND THE BEAUTY IN LIFE AND YOU'LL FIND EVERYTHING

BEAUTIFUL IN YOU

FIND THE BEAUTY IN YOU AND YOU'LL FIND EVERYTHING

BEAUTIFUL IN LIFE

LET ME FALL APART

SOME DAY YOU WILL HAVE HAD ENOUGH

PRAY THERE'S MORE DAYS AHEAD THAN YOU'VE WASTED

LET ME FALL APART

WE EVENTUALLY REALIZE WE KEEP FALLING IN LOVE WITH GHOSTS

LET ME FALL APART

YOU DON'T REALLY KNOW ME

YOU REALLY DON'T KNOW YOU

WE'RE JUST TWO PEOPLE DOING WHAT LOST PEOPLE DO

LET ME FALL APART

WE FILL HOLES WITH EMPTY PROMISES TO OURSELVES

AS WE HOLD ON TO FOREVER BUT WE'RE BLANKETED BY NEVER

JUST BARELY KEEPING OURSELVES TOGETHER

KNOWING WHY THESE TIES NEEDED TO SEVERE

LET ME FALL APART

THOSE WHO KEEP RUNNING BACK TO DRINK THE SAME WATER

NEVER UNDERSTAND THEIR THIRST

LET ME FALL APART

WHEN YOU'VE HAD ENOUGH YOU'LL KNOW

YOU'LL DIVORCE THE PAST

TO SEE YOUR PRESENT

BECAUSE IT'S THE FUTURE THAT YOU OWE

LET ME FALL APART

IF WE TURNED ALL THE WONDERING WHY'S INTO GOODBYES

WE'D GIVE YEARS BACK TO OUR LIVES

LET ME FALL APART

I'D LIKE TO APOLOGIZE

I CANNOT TAKE AWAY THAT PAIN

WHERE YOUR HURT BECAME A GAME

HOW I WISHED I COULD BE

EVERYTHING YOU HAD HOPED OF ME

I CAN SEE YOU STRUGGLING TO SURVIVE

ONCE FULL OF LIFE AND NOW BARELY ALIVE

ALL HOPE SEEMS OUT OF REACH

SOMETIMES LOVE IS JUST HARD TO TEACH

THE BLOOD HAS WASHED AWAY

AS MY HEART IS SOAKED IN BLEACH

LET ME FALL APART

IT IS WHAT IT IS, UNTIL IT ISN'T

KEEP MOVING FOREWARD

EMBRACE THE PUSH & IGNORE THE PULL

YOU'LL EVENTUALLY BE WHERE YOU NEED TO GO

LET ME FALL APART

I USED TO CARE ABOUT EVERYTHING

NOW I CARE ABOUT NOTHING

I'M NOT SURE WHICH IS SCARIER

LET ME FALL APART

I THOUGHT I HAD YOU ALL FIGURED OUT

UNTIL YOU THREW IT ALL AWAY

LET ME FALL APART

WE'RE ALL GONNA DIE SOME DAY

SOME WILL SAY THEY KNEW US

OTHERS THEY LOVED US

BUT MAY THEY ALL MISS US

LET ME FALL APART

FIND AN HONEST LOVE

ONE THAT UNRAVELS ALL YOUR DOUBTS

SEWS UP ALL YOUR OPEN WOUNDS

ROUNDS ALL YOUR SHARP EDGES

AWAKENS YOUR SOUL

FIND THE LOVE THAT NEEDS NO WORDS

AND WHEN YOU DO, YOU NEED TO FIGHT FOR IT WITH ALL YOU HAVE

HOLD ON TO IT TILL YOUR LAST BREATH BREAKS THE AIR

THAT'S AN HONEST LOVE

LET ME FALL APART

YOU CAN PAINT WITH COLOR, BUT THE BLACK & WHITE WILL SHOW

YOU'LL FIND THE TRIP IS OVER LONG BEFORE YOU GO

WORDS NEVER MEAN ANYTHING TO A DEAF EAR

HOLDING AN EMBRACE THAT MEANS NOTHING WHEN NEAR

IT'S JUST A GAME WHERE WE ALL PLAY OUR ROLES

COUNTLESS VICTIMS WHO BARE THEIR SOULS

DEVILS LAUGH AS ANGELS FLY

WE'LL CATCH A TEAR BEFORE WE CRY

LIMITS GIVEN WAY TO THE EMOTIONAL WAR

BLEEDING THE SURFACE TILL YOUR HEART HAS TORE

LOOK IN A MIRROR TO SEE WHAT I SEE

ANOTHER DAY SEARCHING FOR A REASON TO BE

LET ME FALL APART

I MAY HAVE NOT WON YOU BACK

BUT AT LEAST I SHOWED UP TO FIGHT

LET ME FALL APART

AFTER ALL THE PAIN I COULDN'T UNDO

I'M TIRED OF HURTING AS I LIMP AWAY FROM YOU

YOU FAILED TO SEE

THAT YOUR LOVE TOOK THE BEST OF ME

LET ME FALL APART

STOP BLEEDING ON THE PEOPLE WHO DIDN'T CUT YOU

JUST TO RUN BACK TO THE ONE'S STILL HOLDING THE BLADE

LET ME FALL APART

I THOUGHT THE WORLD OF YOU

BUT THE WORLD DIDN'T THINK MUCH OF YOU FOR ME

LET ME FALL APART

ALL THESE WORDS UNSPOKEN

A WISH WON'T FILL THIS SPACE

IF I HAD ANOTHER HOUR OR EVEN A SECOND

JUST TO SEE YOUR FACE

NEVER KNEW IT WOULD BE THE LAST TIME

I'D HOLD ON TO A LOOK A LITTLE LONGER

NOW YOU'RE GONE & IT'S TO LATE

THESE TEARS FALL AS I TRY TO STAY STRONGER

EVEN THOUGH I MAY NEVER SEE YOU AGAIN

ALL THESE MEMORIES I'LL NEVER LET GO

STARING AT THESE OLD PICTURES I SMILE

HOLD ON TO YOUR FRIENDS. BECAUSE YOU NEVER KNOW

LET ME FALL APART

TIME TO RIDE OFF AGAIN

MY LAST SUNSET

TUCK IT AWAY UNDER THE BED

LABELED THINGS WE'LL NEVER SEE AGAIN

LET ME FALL APART

LOYALTY ONLY EXISTS IN THE ABSENCE OF OPPORTUNITY

LET ME FALL APART

THE FIRE MAY HAVE DIED OUT

BUT THE MEMORY STILL BURNS

LET ME FALL APART

THIS LOVE WAS FICTION

WRITTEN ON A PAGE TO WASH AWAY

AS THE SONG WAS NEVER MEANT TO PLAY

A HEARTBEAT LOST IN AN ECHO

ONE LAST BREATH TO BREATHE

SAYING OUR FINAL GOODBYES LONG BEFORE WE LEAVE

PICTURES ARE ALL THAT ARE LEFT

SMILE BECAUSE THE SORROW WILL FADE

PUT THE PAST TO SLEEP & BURY THE PLANS WE MADE

IT'S OVER AND THAT'S OK

NO TIME FOR SORRY OR TO SHED A TEAR

THIS PATH IN LIFE HAS LED US HERE

LET ME FALL APART

I'D RATHER RUN TO THE THINGS THAT SCARE ME

THEN AWAY FROM THE FEAR INSIDE ME

LET ME FALL APART

SOMETIMES I HATE THAT I STILL LOVE YOU

BUT I LOVE THAT I DON'T HATE YOU

LET ME FALL APART

SOMETIMES ALL YOU CAN SAY IS

"I JUST WANTED YOU TO BE OK"

LET ME FALL APART

SOMETIMES YOU NEVER GET ANOTHER DAY WITH SOME PEOPLE

THEY RUN AWAY FROM TODAY

TO ESCAPE TOMORROW

LET ME FALL APART

FINDING OUT WHO WE ARE IS THE BIGGEST SECRET TO LIFE

GO LOOK IN THE MIRROR & IT WILL NEVER LIE TO YOU

SHUT OFF THE OUTSIDE WORLD FOR A DAY, NO NOISE

JUST YOU AND THE FRESH AIR

FIND OUT WHO YOU ARE & WANT TO

LOVE THAT PERSON UNCONDITIONALLY

THAT LIFE YOU WANT WILL COME TO YOU BUT YOU HAVE TO BELEIVE IN YOURSELF

LET ME FALL APART

A WOMAN CONSTANTLY GETS BITTEN BY HER SNAKE AND ASKS IT

"WHY DO YOU ALWAYS BITE ME EVEN WHEN I TAKE CARE OF YOU?"

"I'M A SNAKE IT REPLIED WHAT DID YOU EXPECT?"

LET ME FALL APART

ACCEPT WHAT TODAY IS

AND FORGET WHAT YESTERDAY COULDN'T OFFER

THERE IS NO VALUE IN THE PAST

PUT ALL YOUR ENERGY INTO THE PRESENT

YOU'LL BE AMAZED AT WHAT MAY COME TOMORROW

LET ME FALL APART

I MISS YOU

THE YOU, YOU WERE AFRAID TO BE

THE YOU, YOU WERE WITH ME

THE YOU THAT FELL IN LOVE WITH BEING FREE

LET ME FALL APART

SOMETIMES WE WANT THE CHASE TO BE OVER SO BAD

WE TRY TO BUILD WHEN WE'RE NOT COMPATIBLE WITH THE LAND

GREAT THINGS TAKE TIME & IF YOU DON'T KNOW YOURSELF

THEN EVERYONE ELSE IS JUST PASSING THROUGH

LET ME FALL APART

YOU'LL NEVER LET IN NEW LOVE

UNTIL YOU LET GO OF THE OLD ONE THAT HURT YOU

CHANGE HAPPENS AFTER CLARITY

LOVE HAPPENS WHEN YOU LET GO TO LET IN

LET ME FALL APART

THE DIFFERENCE BETWEEN SOMEBODY AND SOMEONE IS

ANYBODY CAN HAVE A SOMEBODY

BUT IT TAKES A SPECIAL PERSON TO BE SOMEBODY'S SOMEONE

LET ME FALL APART

IT'S NOT THE WORDS THAT DEFINE US

IT'S THE ACTIONS & MOMENTS

ESPECIALLY THE HARD ONES WE THINK WE'LL NEVER GET THROUGH

THEY MAKE US HUMAN AND LET US KNOW WE'LL ENDURE

TO OUR GREATEST ACHIEVEMENTS

BE IT AS FIGHTERS, PARENTS OR LOVERS

LET ME FALL APART

MOST OF THE THINGS WE'VE STOLEN

WERE FROM OURSELVES

LET ME FALL APART

USE YOUR VOICE

RAISE YOUR VOLUME

STAND IN FRONT OF THE CROWD

AND CHANGE THE WORLD

LET ME FALL APART

THE EASIEST WAY TO CONTROL SOMEBODY IS TO GET

THEM TO SECOND GUESS THEIR OWN FEELINGS

LET ME FALL APART

IT'S NOT A SECOND CHANCE IF YOU'RE ON THE SAME BEACH

WATCHING THE SAME STARS AS THE WAVES CRASH

THE SANDS STILL REMEMBERS THE "I LOVE YOU"

THAT WAS WRITTEN ON ITS SKIN

LET ME FALL APART

DO WE GO BACK AND CHASE OLD FEELINGS?

THE ONES THAT KEPT US ALIVE

OR DO WE KEEP LOSING OURSELVES ON

THE EMPTY WORDS PRESENTED TO US

IN THE MONTAGE OF SOMEONE ELSE'S LIFE

NEVER LET YOUR FEAR OF SOMEONE'S WORDS

KEEP YOU FROM SOMEONE ELSE'S LOVE

I KNOW WE ALWAYS SEEM TO LOSE

BUT MAYBE IT'S TIME WE ACTUALLY WON

LET ME FALL APART

LIFE'S FULL OF ORIGINS AND AFTERMATHS

BONFIRES AND ASHES

UPS AND DOWNS

TAKE OFFS AND CRASHES

WE'RE ALL STITCHED TOGETHER WITH RIGHT AND WRONG

WE DANCE TO DIFFERENT RHYTHMS, TO THE SAME SONG

WITH NOTHING BEING EASY THE TRIALS, TRIBULATIONS

AND PATHS THAT AREN'T ALL THE SAME

BE IT WEAK OR STRONG, BLACK OR WHITE WE ALL PLAY THE GAME

LIFE'S FULL OF BONDS AND CLASHES

DARKNESS AND COLOR FLASHES

WE EITHER LEAD OR FOLLOW

BUT IN THE END A GRAVE IS STILL A GRAVE, BE IT DEEP OR SHALLOW

LET ME FALL APART

YOU'RE BIGGEST FAN & HATER WILL BOTH

BE CLAPPING THE LOUDEST

IT ALL DEPENDS ON WHERE THEY'RE SITTING

DURING YOUR WINS & LOSSES

LET ME FALL APART

SOME PEOPLE DON'T WANT ANYTHING BUT YOUR TIME

LET ME FALL APART

ONE OF THE BIGGEST LESSONS IN LIFE IS FIGURING OUT

THE DIFFERENCE BETWEEN "I HAVE TO & I GET TO"

LET ME FALL APART

IT WAS A HIDDEN FEAR

BUT I WAS RIGHT

YOU WERE NEVER REALLY HERE

LET ME FALL APART

DO IT TODAY!

BECAUSE TODAY THERE IS NO TOMORROW

LET ME FALL APART

I DIDN'T NEED YOU IN MY LIFE

I WANTED YOU IN IT

THERE'S A DIFFERNCE

LET ME FALL APART

FALL IN LOVE WITH THE ALLURE OF A BETTER LIFE

LET ME FALL APART

FOR SOME PEOPLE YOU'RE ONLY GOING TO BE A MOMENT IN TIME

DO YOUR BEST TO A GOOD ONE

LET ME FALL APART

ONE OF THE BIGGEST FEARS YOU SHOULD HAVE IN LIFE

IS NOT LIVING A FULL ONE

LET ME FALL APART

HOW DO YOU KNOW IF THE LOVE IS REAL?

WHEN IT HURTS TO THINK OF A LIFE WITHOUT THEM

LET ME FALL APART

NEVER SETTLE FOR ANYTHING LESS THAN YOU DESERVE

BECAUSE YOU DESERVE THE WORLD

LET ME FALL APART

THEY SAY LOOK ON THE BRIGHTSIDE

BUT NEVER TELL YOU WHAT MAY BE LURKING IN THE DARKNESS

LET ME FALL APART

SOMETIMES IT'S OK TO BE SELFISH

SOMETIMES IT'S OK TO DO YOU

DON'T BE APOLOGETIC IN WHAT YOU WANT OUT OF LIFE

LET ME FALL APART

YOUR WORDS HAVE WEIGHT

THEY CARRY VALUE

BE VERY CAREFUL HOW YOU USE THEM

YOU CAN CHANGE A LIFE OR RUIN ONE WITH THEM

LET ME FALL APART

THE SERENDIPITOUS MOMENTS

DRAWING LIFE OUT OF INSPIRATION

AS TRAGEDY SET INTO AN ENDLESS LOVE STORY

WHERE DID I LOSE MYSELF TRYING TO TELL THE TALE

THE WORLDS I LEFT YOU WEREN'T EVER MEANT TO FAIL

LET ME FALL APART

I WONDER IF YOU STILL THINK ABOUT ME AT ALL

I THOUGHT IT WAS SPRINT TO FORGET YOU

BUT I GUESS IT'S A CRAWL

LET ME FALL APART

STOP FORGETTING YOUR VALUE WHEN YOU'RE LONELY

TEMPORY ATTENTION CAN ROB US BLIND

DON'T RUSH OPEN ARMS

HEALING IN WAIT IS PRICELESS

LET ME FALL APART

THE ULTIMATE FAILURE IN LIFE

IS MAKING EVERYONE ELSE HAPPY BUT YOU

LET ME FALL APART

LIKE A 1000 MILE SUNSET FADING INTO THE OCEAN WAVES

WE'RE JUST MAKING MEMORIES ON OUR WAY TO OUR GRAVES

LET ME FALL APART

SOME PEOPLE WERE BORN TO BURN THEIR OWN BRIDGE

OVER A RIVER OF TEARS THEY CRIED

TREAD WATER, TREAD WATER.....DROWN

LET ME FALL APART

WE ALL HAVE SCARS

IT'S HOW WE DISPLAY THEM

THAT DEFINES US

LET ME FALL APART

I'D LIKED TO BELIEVE YOU WEREN'T GONE

THAT YOU WERE JUST LOST

AND I'D SEE YOU AGAIN SOME DAY

LET ME FALL APART

NEVER BURY YOUR SECRETS IN A SHALLOW GRAVE

EVENTUALLY THE SKELETONS REACH THE SURFACE

LET ME FALL APART

NEVER GET SO LOST IN YOURSELF THAT YOU FORGET

YOUR VALUE IN LIFE

OUR SOULS NEED FULL HEARTS TO SURVIVE

LET ME FALL APART

I'M THE PASSENGER SO DRIVE

THE SLOW RIDE TO DEATH KEEPS ME ALIVE

ABOLISHED THIS SELF IMPOSED TRAUMA

BURY ME SIX FEET DOWN SO I CAN ESCAPE THE DRAMA

LET ME FALL APART

NEVER REGRET CREATING A BETTER LIFE

LET ME FALL APART

WE MIGHT NOT HAVE ALL THE ANSWERS

BUT PART OF OUR JOURNEY IS SEARCHING FOR THEM

LET ME FALL APART

THE JOURNEY BEGINS WITH A WORD

A COMPLEX STORY UNTOLD

SIMPLE TO THE EYES YET UNOPENED TO SEE

THE MAP TO LIFE HIDES WITHIN OUR HEARTS

LET ME FALL APART

IT'S MY JOB TO PROTECT MY HEART

IT'S YOUR JOB TO PRESERVE IT

LET ME FALL APART

THIS BOOK IS DEDICATED TO

THE LOVING MEMORY OF JAMES LAYAYETTE

THANK YOU FOR BEING MY BIGGEST FAN

AND ALWAYS BELIEVING IN ME

Made in the USA
Middletown, DE
17 March 2024